the Grief Cure

the Grief Cure

*A Revolutionary Guide to
Healing from Loss*

ALYSON FRANZ

NEW YORK

LONDON • NASHVILLE • MELBOURNE • VANCOUVER

the Grief Cure

A Revolutionary Guide to Healing from Loss

© 2020 Alyson Franz

Published in New York, New York, by Morgan James Publishing in partnership with Difference Press. Morgan James is a trademark of Morgan James, LLC. www.MorganJamesPublishing.com

ISBN 9781642794069 paperback
ISBN 9781642794076 eBook
ISBN 9781642794083 audiobook
Library of Congress Control Number: 2018914552

Cover Design by:
Rachel Lopez
www.r2cdesign.com

Interior Design by:
Christopher Kirk
www.GFSstudio.com

Morgan James is a proud partner of Habitat for Humanity Peninsula and Greater Williamsburg. Partners in building since 2006.

Get involved today! Visit
MorganJamesPublishing.com/giving-back

For my Dad. This book would not have been possible without his love and dedication to me in the first 29 years of my life.

Table of Contents

Introduction

Feeling held back by grief is a hard place to be. I've been there. Searching for answers. Knowing that answers exist but having no idea where to find them. It took me over a year of pain to start manifesting the solution to heal my broken heart.

What I've learned on my journey of healing from this pain has been priceless. To think that all of that misery could lead to something positive and good is far beyond anything I could have fathomed at the beginning of my journey. In my mind, my worst nightmare had occurred. I lost my dad who was my main source of love in this world. How could anything positive ever come from that? It was far beyond my comprehension.

What I didn't expect to find was that there was a purpose to that pain. My mortal mind, wanting things to be comfortable and "my way," couldn't comprehend that something so difficult could actually have value. No one had ever told me that good things can come from things that are painful. So I had no idea it was even possible.

When I think of everything I went through on this journey, one of the most important life lessons I've gotten is to realize that good things come out of everything that happens in life. Whether or not it seems that way. We often judge what's happening and label it as bad, which makes it impossible to see the value that it can have in our life.

At the beginning of my journey, all I wanted was for life to be normal again. To make it through the day without a crying spell, being irritated with the world, and sleep through the night. But what I got was so much more than that.

Everything in our life is intended for our soul's growth, and if we can keep that in mind – regardless of how it may appear on the surface – we will grow and use these life experiences according to the Divine curriculum that created them.

Although I love my father dearly and always will, I now understand our relationship in a deeper way and I understand why it had to change form at the time that it did.

The pain from the loss of my dad was what broke me open and made me willing to look at life in a whole different way. The more we suffer, the more we become willing to get off the wrong track and onto the right one.

When I first started working with Kristin, she was in a similar place. She was upset almost all of the time, overreacting to anything in her life that didn't go her way. She would fluctuate from insomnia to oversleeping and both would affect her job on a daily basis.

Her marriage went into turmoil, and her young children were starting to show negative behaviors. While she wanted to make changes so she could succeed at work and save her marriage, once she saw how her emotional struggles were affecting her children, she realized that she had to find a way to heal. Her kids dissolved all of the ambivalence she had about getting better.

Kristin was willing to do whatever it took to be the healthy mother that her children deserve to have. After working with Kristin for some time now, I'm really proud of all she has accomplished. Life has turned out to be much better than she ever expected! Everything has fallen into place for her, and more! Stay tuned for more about Kristin's story in Chapter 1 so you can hear more about the great things that are happening for her now.

My own healing process in this journey also turned out to be invaluable. I now consider it to be my mission to help everyone who is suffering from a traumatic loss to be able to heal their heart completely, understand why they are going through this suffering, and rebuild their life in a way that makes them feel unshakable in the face of life, never to feel powerless over their emotions again.

If you are suffering from loss, this book is for you. You don't need to suffer. Life is not meant to be miserable. It's meant to be fun, happy, and peaceful! I promise that you have the power to shift into the emotional state and mindset you need to be able to heal from this tragic loss completely.

My hope is to completely change the way that the world views grief so that people can start truly healing from this devastating experience. The world is ready for a Paradigm Shift regarding what is possible when faced with this problem. And I hope my book is an instrument for this change.

I'm grateful for this opportunity to share my ideas that will help you heal to your core and start changing the consciousness of the world on this issue. It might be hard to imagine that you can shift out of this pain, but this book will teach you exactly how to do it.

Chapter 1

Meet Kristin

Kristin is a 34-year-old mom of two children who lost her father about 9 months ago. But a year ago, her life was going pretty smooth. She enjoyed teaching her 5th grade class. On weekends, she would take her children on excursions accompanied by her father because her husband was usually working. Her father had an awesome relationship with her kids and it seemed to distract them from the fact that their father rarely played with them.

Her children looked forward to being with their grandfather, wrestling with him, and asking him unusual questions that he seemed to love answering. They looked forward to the weekends and would ask their mother in the mornings, "Is today going to be a Papa Fun Day?" And if the answer was yes, which it usually was, they would jump out of bed and couldn't get ready fast enough for their day.

Kristin and her father had always been close. Kristin's parents divorced when she was 5 and her father received custody of her and her younger sister Alex. Growing up with a dad instead of a mom wasn't her preference and, at times, she felt like the odd one out, but looking back on it as an adult, she wouldn't have wanted it any other way. She occasionally communicates with her mother, but never really bonded with her as she was rarely available to Kristin and her sister in their earlier years.

Kristin had no idea that she would lose her dad so suddenly. He had such a clear desire to be with her and the kids. He loved life and seemed carefree. He surely didn't fit the profile of someone who was at the end of their life.

He was 60 years old, and considered himself to be in perfect health! He was admitted to the hospital for the first time ever because he was having abdominal pain that turned out to be appendicitis and he needed to have his appendix removed. But lots of people have their appendix removed with no complications and continue on to live for decades after the surgery. Unfortunately, it turned out that her dad wasn't in the perfect health that he claimed to be in, and after his surgery, he went downhill quickly. Kristin was in disbelief of what was happening.

One complication after another, the doctors gave her and her sister more and more bad news. They were both sad and in disbelief. So much had changed in such a short time. A few weeks into his hospital stay, Kristin's father died.

When Kristin got the news, she was devastated. And she knew that her kids would be devastated too. He had promised her kids a family vacation to Walt Disney World later that year. Her six-year-old daughter Sophia was already talking daily about meeting the princesses. Her four-year-old son Bentley was an animal lover and would talk excitedly at least once a week about seeing the elephants and giraffes. Now the trip couldn't happen because she was depending on her dad to be with her and the kids on the trip.

Not only did she have to break the news to her children that they are not going to Disney, she had to explain to them that there won't be any more "Papa Fun Days" ever again. She was sure that this was the worst day of her life. And this was only the beginning.

Despite Kristin believing that this was the worst day of her life, she was hoping very much that she and the kids would get over this hump quicker and easier than expected. But that wasn't the case. If anything, it was actually worse than she had expected.

The loss of her father meant that Kristin now had to raise and entertain her children by herself. Her father was her co-parent and best friend. Sure, she has a husband who is their father, but since he was promoted in his company two years ago, he's barely been available to his family. Initially, Kristin supported this position because the long hours were expected to be temporary. However, she can now see that it's not temporary. She has asked him to step down from his management position so he can spend more time with his family, but he has said no, rationalizing his long hours because of his large salary.

To make matters worse, now, nine months later, the children still ask Kristin when they're going to see Papa again. They can't fathom that their Papa would ever leave them. Their question reminds Kristin of how much she too misses her father. And she also feels like she can never answer this question right, because she herself isn't sure what she believes.

Kristin was still grieving deeply. She would get angry and upset several times daily. She overreacted to almost anything in her life that didn't go her way. She had sleep problems and could barely function at work most days, arriving late almost daily. Her marriage was in turmoil and her kids had begun to show negative behaviors that were very out of character for them.

She didn't know what to do about her emotional state and all of the problems it was clearly creating. She tried going to a mental health therapist. But she would just cry through the sessions, which seemed to make her feel worse.

So she started reading self-help books looking for a solution. She learned a lot in her reading and came across many great ideas. But she had a really hard time following through and implementing what she had learned.

Finally, she confided in a friend what she was going through and they referred her to me. She was relieved to know that I've helped many people transform unbearable emotional states just like hers into total peace and happiness.

When Kristin first started working with me, almost everything I taught her were brand-new concepts. And the healing work we did together was more comprehensive than anything she'd come across prior as well.

She had read so many self-help books in the six months before she met me, she was surprised that the helpful knowledge I shared with her were concepts she had never come across before. And they worked for her, like magic actually. (Most of my clients see a dramatic improvement in 2-4 months, but Kristin started turning around after just 1 month!)

Kristin started seeing amazing changes in every area of her life in just one month. In fact, she was so amazed at what we accomplished in our first two months together, she signed up to work with me for a full year after her two-month program had ended.

The year that we worked together was an amazing year for her. Everything in her life totally changed, even things that she didn't know she wanted to change got better!

"How is Kristin doing now?" you might be wondering. Kristin is doing fabulous! She was promoted at work, her marriage is better than it has ever been, her kids are happy every day, and she's started training to be a life coach! She feels that what she learned in our year together was so incredibly valuable, that she wants to be able to share it with others in her own unique way.

Why Kristin's Emotional Pain Ran Deep

Kristin believed that her life was going pretty smooth one year ago, but actually it wasn't. Her dad was just the glue holding together the mediocre pieces of her life.

Let's break it down:

Kristin got married seven years ago to a man that has always provided for her and her children financially, but had never been emotionally available to her. And in the past two years, he hadn't been physically available to her either. She had tried to talk to him about this but he would shut down or say that he's too stressed about work to talk to her about these issues. Having her dad in the picture allowed her to avoid communicating with her husband about her feelings of loneliness within their marriage.

In fact, Kristin actually questioned whether her husband even loved her anymore. She certainly didn't feel loved by him. She didn't feel like she had a partner. And they hadn't gone out on a date in almost 3 years.

Kristin teaches 5th grade at a local elementary school. She's great at it, and everyone can see what a talented teacher she is. But deep down in her heart, she's not fulfilled by this career. She is incredibly dedicated to her students and her school, so on the surface you'd think she has acquired her dream job. But that's just her love for humanity and hard-working nature.

She thought about moving to a higher position in the school but, being unsure that she even wanted to be in the education field, she was ambivalent. Her work schedule was convenient for raising children and, because they were her priority, that was the deciding factor.

Kristin's only hobby was taking the kids out on weekends with her father. She used to go to the gym and enjoy working out, but her husband being consumed by work all day prevented her from having any free time to herself because she's always with her children.

Kristin had two close friends who she rarely saw because she was consumed by work and raising her children. She wanted to connect with them more, but never seemed to find the time.

Kristin had also suffered with anxiety in the past, had sleep problems and migraine headaches regularly for a few years before her father passed.

Not to mention, she hadn't been on a vacation in 5 years.

So, despite what Kristin thought her life was before her father passed, when you take a close look at it, it actually wasn't that great. I would call it mediocre at best. However, having the love and support of her dad made up for all of the voids in her uncomfortable and unsatisfied life and it allowed her to stay in a pretty uncomfortable comfort zone.

She knew that she could count on her dad to be there for her unconditionally, which made her life very easy. Therefore, she didn't have to deal with any of the deeper issues in her life that were bothering her beneath the surface.

Kristin's Comfort Zone

Kristin wasn't actually happy in her life – she was just comfortable. Having the support of her dad felt great, and it was not just because he was an awesome and loving father and grandfather. It was also because having him in her life created a buffer to cover over all of the unhappiness and unfulfillment she was experiencing in her life overall. Having his support made her happy and comfortable enough that she didn't have to look at any of these deeper issues in her life.

Just like Kristin, we all have a comfort zone, and we usually end up staying in it unless something pushes us out of it. And usually it's some type of trauma, experience, or life event. In Kristin's case, the pain of her grief ran deep, which made her willing to do whatever it took to make the necessary changes in her life.

As they say in Zen Buddhism, we learn two ways: through pain or through awakening.

In Kristin's case, she learned from her pain AND awakened!

Aspects and Origins of Pain from a Traumatic Loss

The pain of Kristin's loss comes from multiple aspects of her situation.

The primary aspects are:

1. Kristin lost her father, who was also her best friend, co-parent, and source of love
2. Kristin lost her comfort zone, which she did not want to leave

3. Kristin lost her emotional stability
4. Kristin felt loss on behalf of her children despite them not actually understanding death

Despite having these multiple aspects of pain, the origin of her pain all came from one source: Her inner reaction to all of these aspects.

I often refer to grief that is disruptive and has lasted longer than one year as "Traumatic Grief" because that indicates that the grief you're experiencing is resonating in your body in a way that is similar to a trauma.

Inner Reactions

All of our experiences in life are seen through a unique filter that is personal to us. We rarely – if ever – see anything as it actually "is." But that comes with being human. We are rarely neutral in what we experience, and that non-neutrality can greatly color the way we view a situation.

This non-neutral way of viewing our situations leads to the way we think about them. Our thoughts about them lead to our feelings about them. And when we feel bad about something, guess what? We have even more negative thoughts about it.

Many people, including society in general, view particular types of experiences similarly. This can lead us to forget that we actually have the freedom to choose to see something differently from the way others see it. We have the ability to think outside of what you could consider the societal norm's way of thinking.

And our well-meaning loved ones often feed into the perspective of how difficult a situation is rather than trying to cheer us up, which can make it even harder to see things differently.

But the reality is that we actually have a lot of freedom about how we choose to see things. We have the power to change our thoughts and perspective any time we choose. Owning your power to choose the way you view situations in your life can help you to start shifting into new possibilities that you didn't even know were there.

"In the world, you will have tribulation. But take heart; I have overcome the world."

In this quote by Jesus of Nazareth, I believe that he is referring to our freedom to choose how we see and deal with the more difficult things in life.

The other part of your inner reaction is your bodily response to an experience. Those negative thoughts and emotions produce a charge in your body's energy system that makes it easy to continue reproducing them. This negative charge is actually the root cause of your grief and negative perceptions. This is also why traditional talk therapy and medication don't heal grief. You need to shift your body's energy system to release the energetic charge. The good news is, that once you release the negative charges, you will release your emotional pain as well.

Kristin was surprised to learn just how much negative charge she was carrying about the loss of her father, and as we worked on releasing the negative charge, her emotional state and other areas of her life began shifting quickly and her life perspectives began changing naturally. She began to develop a deep sense of peace in just a very short time.

Chapter 2

My Story

Back in my late 20s, I thought life was great. I was traveling often, spending lots of time in Mexico, learning Latin Dance, and hanging out with my friends several times a week. I was self-employed, single, and enjoying life. I didn't care that I didn't have a steady dating partner or a career that I loved. I was having fun, and as far as I was concerned, my dad and my brother were my family unit. So why would I need a steady partner or a career that I truly loved? In my mind – I was doing just fine!

My father had been ill for many years with a rare auto-immune disease that most people haven't heard of. When he was diagnosed in the mid-90s, we were told that he probably wouldn't live much longer. But 10 years later, he seemed to be plugging along just fine, so we threw that theory out the window. Sure, he walked with a cane and some days he didn't feel good, but lots of people live that way for decades.

So that night in late October in 2009, as I was packing my bags and chatting with friends – preparing for my trip – a week-long Dance Excursion in The Dominican Republic that I was planning to leave for the next day, the last thing in the world that I imagined happening was getting a phone call that my father had a massive heart-attack and the paramedics were trying to resuscitate him, but the situation didn't look good.

Needless to say, my trip was canceled and my life went spiraling in a completely different direction. I didn't go out dancing for the entire first month because I spent most of my days crying and depressed.

The night my father passed, I didn't sleep, and that was also the onset of a battle with insomnia that I would deal with for a few years. I felt needy, miserable, and irritated so often, I felt like I didn't know myself. I'd never been this way. I just wanted things to go back to the way that they were. On multiple occasions, I wished my life was just a nightmare that I'd wake up from.

And to make matters worse, all of the PTSD symptoms related to child abuse I experienced that I'd gone to therapy for years prior had come back. My mother was again acting abusively toward me and her behavior brought back the emotional pain I experienced in childhood.

Add to that – my younger brother was 16 at the time, super traumatized by the loss and facing other challenges in his life at the same time. He was used to being with my dad pretty much all day every day.

My life was a mess. I was a mess. I couldn't imagine life getting worse than what it was at that particular time. I was afraid that if one more major stressor happened – I really might lose my mind.

After several months of being in this state with almost no improvement, I reluctantly turned to psychotherapy. Being a therapist myself at the time, I knew the limits of what talk therapy could accomplish and really didn't think it would be a solution. But I was desperate, so I gave it a try.

I found a therapist who was trained in "EMDR" (Eye Movement Desensitization Reprocessing). This is a special trauma treatment method, known to be more helpful than just traditional talk therapy for treating trauma issues. It didn't work. My therapist was a wonderful person, well-trained, and really wanted to help me. But it just didn't work. After almost a year of weekly sessions, I felt no noticeable change in my symptoms. She suggested I try medication, but I refused because I knew it was not the solution to my problem.

I was frustrated that I hadn't found a solution, but deep down I knew that there had to be one. So I googled. And waited. Deep in my heart I knew something would come along. But I didn't know when, or what it would be. So I just kept up my faith that it would appear.

A few months later, I received a flyer in the mail for a training that would be held in Boston, Massachusetts in the spring. It was from a psychologist in New York City named Henry Grayson. The flyer read "Revolutionary Methods for Health and Healing" and went into details about how it would include a fusion of "Energy Psychology" methods and many other healing modalities as well. I knew in my gut that this was it. I *had* to attend this training no matter what. There was something about this flyer that felt magical and had infinite possibilities in it. I was deeply drawn to it.

I attended this 2-day training and was amazed by what I learned. The concepts that Henry taught were so different from anything I'd ever heard in my life, but deep down I just knew they were true, and I needed more training with this man who had tapped into something completely outside of the world's paradigm. I went home from the training using as many of these new concepts as I could, both on myself and with my clients. I was eager to train with him again in the fall, as he had given his word that he would come back to Boston to train us again at that time.

When he came back in the fall, this second training was more in-depth and we received more hands-on experience. On the 2nd day of the training, I experienced a healing that was so profound that I could feel something inside me shift and a deep new inner peace start to develop. Some of the emotional pain deep inside of me had released. I went home that night and had my first full night of sleep in almost two years. To me this was a sign. I needed to do a lot of this work on myself, and I also needed to learn it really well so I could share it with the world. There was something about this experience that felt very different and special. And I knew in my gut that the world needed as much of this type of healing as it could get!

That Monday after the training, I called Henry and told him that I wanted to be his client. Despite the fact that his two offices were three hours from my home, I had the will and would find a way to get to one of his offices as frequently as possible. To my surprise, he recommended I work with his colleague who was slightly closer to my area. I was grateful for this suggestion, because saving time on my commute there would mean I'd have to take less time out of work and might even be able to go there more often. (In 2011, when this conversation occurred, video call platforms such as Skype and Zoom were not widely used for therapy, as they are now.)

Shortly after beginning my work with Henry's colleague Linda, I realized that I had a lot of deep inner work that needed to be done. It was not just the loss of my dad that needed to heal. It was also the loss of everything that my dad provided in my life that I was depending on him for because I was not providing it for myself.

The love that I felt from my dad glazed over the wounds of deep emotional pain that I had no idea I was carrying and was desperately in need of healing. Much of this pain was from multiple forms of abuse I had suffered in my early years. His love distracted me from all of the negative beliefs I had about marriage and relationships from the domestic violence and dysfunction that I witnessed growing up. It distracted me from realizing that I had lost all faith in finding a fulfilling romantic relationship after the ending a five-year relationship in my early 20s. And most of all, he was a source of love outside myself that I very much needed, because on the inside I was barely loving myself at all.

Upon these realizations, I felt overwhelmed with how much work I needed to do to get where I needed to be. And it was apparent within just a few months of working with Linda. But after each session, I could feel the power of my energy shifting. I could feel myself manifesting opportunities and experiences that didn't usually come along to me. And if these new opportunities and experiences could start appearing in my life after just a few months of doing this work, imagine what could happen if I stick with this work? In a few years, my life just might be unrecognizable. I knew in my heart that this was the way to let go of anything in my life that was holding me back from the peace and joy that I had just begun to realize was possible. I became committed to making my life better than it had ever been.

Over the next five years, I made growth and healing a priority in my life. I worked with Linda intensively and I became a personal growth junky – hungry to learn new information and techniques that could better my life or help me to better the world. And I began walking down a spiritual path that would change my life forever.

The decision to dedicate those five years to my healing and growth is the best decision that I've ever made in my life. Every area of my life has completely transformed in ways that I never imagined possible. And the sense of inner peace, clarity, and trust that I have on a daily basis is invaluable and has made me unshakable in the face of life. I no longer fear "something bad happening" because I now know that everything in the world is driven by an intelligence much higher than my own.

Now, I can honestly say, crazy as it may sound, that the loss of my dad and the pain that I had to go through in order to heal makes sense to me. And I'm actually grateful for it. The pain forced me to examine myself and my life in deep and honest ways that I would never have done if I had not been so uncomfortable. It was only in my desperation that I was willing to change. I'm now grateful for that desperation, because without it, I probably wouldn't have changed. I'd probably still be living in the dull pain I was experiencing in my late 20s, unconscious to who I am and what I'm here to do. There is no growth in life without discomfort.

One of my favorite quotes about the value of discomfort is by Rebecca Campbell in her "Letter to a Lightworker" where she says, "I believe that your tragedies, your losses, your sorrows, your hurt happened for you not to you. And I bless the thing that broke you down and cracked you open because the world needs you open." I now believe that's the purpose of emotional pain. To open us up so we can awaken to our True Self.

In this letter, Rebecca addresses people who have a high calling in life, also known as Lightworkers. She believes that Lightworkers don't always recognize themselves for who they are because they become consumed with their pain or think that they are on the wrong track. But both being in pain

AND off track can be exactly what you need to get on the right track. In fact, she also says in this letter, "I believe that you are more on track than you feel – especially if you don't feel it. For the further you get off track, the closer you are to abandoning the wrong one and leaping over to the right one."

I had gone so far off track that I was ready to abandon this path that was not working for me. It took me going into a deep dark place, that seemingly had no way out, to be willing to do *anything* to never be there again. And it was there that I began transformation.

One of the most important lessons that I've learned in this lifetime is that deep emotional pain – especially traumatic grief – may very well be used as a tool to spring you into personal transformation. And it is in this transformation that you truly begin to live.

Why I Created a Program to Heal from Traumatic Grief

Our power to heal from traumatic grief is a gift, and many people don't know that we have this important power. The pain of traumatic grief can be profound, and not everyone understands the purpose of profound emotional pain. There was a time when I certainly didn't understand its purpose. But it is essential to release this pain so you can better understand your Self and the purpose of the grief.

From my own personal journey and struggles, I have come to believe that everything that happens in the Universe is based on an algorithm to help us in our life. But as humans, our mortal minds usually don't comprehend the algorithm. And this is a huge challenge for us, especially when faced with adversity.

When the algorithm isn't aligned with what we want to happen, or it doesn't make sense to us, we assume that something bad has happened. But that's rarely the case, if ever. In some cases, we even draw the conclusion that we did something to deserve this bad thing that happened, which adds a feeling of guilt that clouds our vision even further.

I can assure you that the Universe is driven by a force of love that knows no guilt. All of the great religions of the world acknowledge the importance of forgiveness and I believe that is why. There is no value in guilt. And forgiveness includes forgiving yourself.

When we label something that has occurred as bad, we are making a judgment that limits our vision of what's possible. When we limit our vision, we limit possibilities. This makes it harder for the Universe to do its job for us.

This doesn't mean that you have to like what happened. You might wish with all your heart that this didn't occur. But if you can open to the possibility that just *maybe* the Universe is not random or unintelligent, your life just might start shifting for the better dramatically. And I totally get it that this might sound impossible or downright crazy right now. But if you can stick with me, I promise it will start to make more sense.

I believe it is due to the very high intelligence of the Universe that we often can't comprehend the ways that is helping us even when we might think that it's hurting us.

I believe that there is a huge need in the heart of humanity to be able to understand life and its purpose in a more clear and comprehensive way.

This is why I am willing to share these very personal viewpoints that some people might think are crazy or controversial.

This is why I created a program so you can heal to your core and use this experience to make your life better than it has ever been. I was stuck in this pain for almost two years before I started to find the answers I needed to heal. I don't want anyone to have to be stuck in pain and looking for answers in the dark. I've been there and done that. I want others to benefit from what I learned. No need to reinvent the wheel!

The Grief Cure Program is a powerful system based on what I learned about traumatic grief and transformation on my own personal journey. It can help anyone fully recover from their emotional pain and start transforming into their best life ever. Turn to Chapter 3 and let's start!

Chapter 3

Your Power to Heal

Your body is designed to heal itself. If you fall and scrape your knee, the scrape will heal. And that scrape is no different than any other physical or emotional issue in your life. Some issues will heal on their own. Some will need TLC. And some will need specific treatment and/or knowledge to be cured.

When we look at a problem like a tumor, Western Medicine knows what to do with it because a tumor exists on the physical plane. Western Medicine believes that you need form to change form, which means that a treatment like medication or surgery can cure the tumor. The medication or instruments used in surgery can dissolve or remove the tumor. But problems that are not on the physical plane are often not solved by the western medicine model.

Grief is not on the physical plane. It's on the spiritual

plane. It is an emotion that comes from the soul and isn't clearly seen with the eye, so it requires a deep understanding of what it is in order to heal it. The human race as a whole doesn't have a deep understanding of what grief is, much less our doctors who are trained from an agnostic framework.

Grief has a way of bringing up all of the dull pains that you weren't paying any attention to and making them tender to the touch. That's why all of those smaller upsets and irritations in life that never used to bother you now suddenly do. Healing these underlying wounds is part of healing the grief.

The Grief CURE Program

From my own experience, and from working with dozens of clients, I've found that profound healing from grief comes in four steps. These are:

C – Consciously know and believe in your power to heal

U – Use energy psychology to clear grief from your traumatic losses

R – Revitalize your self-love and spirituality

E – Envision a transformed life and take action

You can begin your healing right now.

Step 1: C – Consciously Know and Believe in Your Power to Heal

Trauma, Fear, and Belief Systems

The experience of traumatic grief requires a deep understanding of it in order to heal because we often develop fears and negative beliefs related to the loss. We may feel scared by the experience, so we draw conclusions about what happened in an attempt to prevent another similar experience from happening. However, the conclusions aren't helpful because they add to the pain associated with the trauma. And just like the trauma, these limiting beliefs and fears also need to be released.

Traditional talk therapy is often unhelpful in cases of traumatic grief (and other trauma) because talking about your experience can strengthen the discomfort. Discussing these issues in-depth without using your body's energetic pathways to release them can result in re-traumatization of an individual or developing more fears and limiting beliefs about the situation as the person replays their experience over and over again.

Trauma, fear, and related belief systems are all interconnected and can be intertwined. The way this can happen is by the conclusions we draw from the experience. These conclusions can lead to negative thoughts about the experience.

These thoughts will often become beliefs. These negative or limiting beliefs about what happened create fear and other negative emotions that add to the pain of what we were already feeling.

Traumatic Grief / Stress can lead to →

Negative Beliefs from the experience (aka Conclusions) →

Which Lead to Negative Thought Patterns →

Which lead to Negative Perceptions →

That Lead to Fear and Negative Emotions →

That lead to Unwanted Symptoms (i.e. insomnia, crying, sadness, upset)

Two examples of how this may manifest for someone experiencing grief:

Traumatic Experience: Sudden Loss of my Father

→Conclusion Belief: My life will never be happy again

→Developed Fear as Result: Fear of never being happy again

Traumatic Experience: Losing My Mother to Cancer

→Conclusion Belief #1: All good people die too early

→Developed Fear as a Result #1: Fear of all my loved ones dying too early

→Conclusion Belief #2: We are powerless over disease

→Developed Fear as a Result #2: Fear of having no control over my health

In order to be free of your grief, you need to be free of the beliefs and fears that are a result of the trauma as well. Otherwise you won't be completely free of it. In some cases, the beliefs or fears may be subconscious, so you will need to access your subconscious in order to identify them.

There are many ways to access your subconscious mind. In my practice, I usually use a process called Applied Kinesiology, also known as "Muscle Testing."

Applied Kinesiology is a method of diagnosis and treatment used in holistic medicine based on the belief that by testing for strength and weakness in certain muscle groups, we are able to identify origins of a medical problem.

This process was originally introduced in 1964 by a chiropractor named George Goodheart, and in the late 1970s a psychologist named Roger Callahan adapted the original discovery so it could be used to access the unconscious mind.

The Importance of Accessing the Subconscious

It's important to access the subconscious when clearing energetic disturbances such as trauma, fears, and beliefs for two main reasons.

The first reason is, in accessing the unconscious, you are able to determine if you have any barriers to releasing the disturbance. Barriers can slow down the clearing process and, in some cases, they can prevent it from happening at all. So it's important to know if there are any barriers present.

One of the most common barriers that I see in my practice is around safety. Our unconscious mind wants to hold on to the problem because it thinks that having the problem makes us safe. Consciously, we know this is not true, otherwise we would not want to clear it in the first place! But our unconscious mind has a tendency to hold on to the things we don't want, thinking that it is protecting us when it is actually creating harm.

The second reason that it's very important to access the subconscious is to make sure that the identified issues are completely cleared. This is very important, otherwise issues that you may think are actually resolved are still present to some degree and they may reactivate at a later time.

In cases of grief, there's a third reason to access the subconscious. The third reason is because of the way that loss is stored in your mind. What you're grieving now may have energetic ties to a loss earlier in life. If that occurs, it's important to work on both of the losses.

I know this process may sound technical or complicated, but I assure you it's not. You have the power to heal safely and easily. I see people do it every day. And if you choose to work with a qualified practitioner, you won't even have to think about these details. And you will probably start seeing results quickly.

The Law of Healing

There are many Universal Laws that I like to refer to when teaching people about self-healing and letting go of blocks. I will refer to a few of them in this book. The first law I'm going to tell you about is the Universal Law of Healing.

According to the Law of Healing, we have two basic emotions. These two emotions are love and fear. Love is the core emotion for all of your positive emotions and Fear is the core emotion for all of your negative emotions.

The Law of Healing believes that all of your issues exist as a result of fear energy replacing the energy of love that naturally flows through your body. As you release the fear, its low vibrational frequency is released and healing starts to take place. Higher-frequency love-based energy will be able to better flow through your body when the fear is released.

The Law of Healing supports the results that I see in my clients daily. We identify the root causes of their issues, release the trauma and fear-based emotions, and they begin shifting into higher emotional frequencies. In cases of grief like Kristin's, the trauma that we released is the trauma of losing her father. She also had a loss earlier in life that was tied to the loss of her father and we cleared that one also.

You have the power to release your trauma and get the same magnificent results that she did!

> *"Love in your mind produces love in your life. This is the meaning of Heaven. Fear in your mind produces fear in your life. This is the meaning of hell."*
> – Marianne Williamson

The Story of The Golden Buddha

In 1957, a monastery in Thailand was relocating to make room for a new highway. The monks arranged for a crane to come and move the 10 foot tall, 2.5 ton clay Buddha to the new location. When the crane started to lift the statue, it was much heavier than expected and it began to crack. In order to protect it, the monks lowered it back down and decided to wait until the next day to bring better equipment. Then, it began raining, so the monks covered it with tarps to keep it dry.

In the middle of night, one of the monks decided to check on the statue to make sure it was well protected. He used a flashlight and went under the tarp to see its condition. From the light of the flashlight shining into one of the cracks in the clay, he saw a glimmer. There was something shining underneath the clay. He started to carefully chisel away the clay and the glimmer grew brighter. Many hours later, all the clay had been removed and he had a Buddha made of solid gold!

Historians believe that this Golden Buddha was covered with clay hundreds of years prior to protect it from an invasion by the Burmese Army. Unfortunately, the Burmese Army won the battle and the monks who knew what was under the clay were killed. So no one knew the truth about this beautiful statue for almost 300 years.

I believe this story is a perfect metaphor for who we are as human beings. Deep down we are magnificent people, but often that's covered up by issues we are carrying on the surface. By tapping into your body's ability to heal and let go of blocks, you step further and further into your magnificent Self who is the Truth of who you are.

Our Deepest Fear

One of my favorite quotes about our True potential is by Marianne Williamson. Many people are acquainted with the first few lines of this quote, but I like to look at the passage in its entirety.

"Our deepest fear is not that we are inadequate.

> *Our deepest fear is that we are powerful beyond*
> *measure. It is our light not our darkness that most*
> *frightens us. We ask ourselves, who am I to be brilliant,*
> *gorgeous, talented and fabulous? Actually, who are you*
> *not to be? You are a child of God. Your playing small*
> *does not serve the world. There's nothing enlightened*
> *about shrinking so that other people won't feel insecure*
> *around you. We were born to make manifest the glory*
> *of God that is within us. It's not just in some of us;*
> *it's in everyone. And as we let our own light shine,*
> *we unconsciously give other people permission to do*
> *the same. As we are liberated from our own fear, our*
> *presence automatically liberates others."*

On a very deep level, we know that we are powerful beings, meant to play big in life and live our full potential. But it's easy to just coast through life because that's what most people do. However, we always have a choice about which path we go down. If you choose to be brave and align with the special path that is meant for you in this lifetime, you will light the path for countless others as well.

When you make a conscious decision to heal from this loss you are experiencing, it's a powerful one. By stepping into this power, you take a stand for yourself and actively acknowledge that you are not at the effect of your circumstances. And that change in perception can do wonders for both your life and the lives around you.

Think about this for a minute: How often do we as a society choose passivity and take no action to amend our circumstances? Imagine if we all started taking action instead. A world full of victors and no victims would be a great place to live.

By consciously knowing and believing that you have the power to heal, you have taken the first step to creating your new world.

Chapter 4

Two Minds

We have two main parts to our mind. Our Conscious and Subconscious Mind. Our conscious mind is the part we use to go through our daily life. Our subconscious mind is in charge of our automatic responses. A good example of how we use our subconscious mind daily is driving home from work every day. We don't need directions, because the route is stored in our mind.

Along with our daily routines, lots of other information is stored in our Subconscious as well. Everything we've ever experienced in our life is stored in our subconscious mind. What did you have for breakfast on May 24, 1996? The answer is in your subconscious. It records everything you experience and has a huge impact on your life because 95% of your behavior is driven by this part of your mind.

It might be hard to believe that 95% of our behavior is driven by the subconscious, but if you can stick with me here, it does make sense.

Think about when we say we want to accomplish something, but we delay it, or don't do it at all. That means our conscious mind and subconscious mind are out of alignment. Your conscious mind wants to do it, but somewhere deep down in your mind's programming, it is saying not to do it. Consciously you want to accomplish it, but unconsciously your mind is not allowing it. So your behavior is going against what you say you want because of the misalignment between your conscious and subconscious.

In working with my clients, especially at the beginning, they are usually amazed by how many beliefs and fears are affecting their daily life that were completely subconscious.

In fact, one client that I worked with recently, Jill, had tons of subconscious beliefs that were affecting her ability to run her business successfully. She came to me feeling like there was a missing piece as to why she wasn't taking action in her business as she should be. Sure enough, by using Applied Kinesiology to access her subconscious we found loads of fears and beliefs that were holding her back.

After we found each fear and belief, we cleared them using Energy Psychology. After each week of clearing, she started to notice that she was feeling lighter and taking more action in her business. Now, she is moving forward in her endeavors and her business is growing with ease.

Step 2: U – Use Energy Psychology to Clear Grief from Your Traumatic Losses

Shifting Inner Reactions

When you enter into the healing process with the intention to start shifting into positive, love-based emotions, working with your body's energy system to start releasing the negative charges that you are experiencing is a good way to start. This will not only help you to release the root cause of your pain, it will help you to naturally start shifting your perception of what is happening in your life which will give you wisdom on how to move forward. Comprehensive Energy Psychology is one method that can definitely help you to accomplish this.

You might be wondering right now what Energy Psychology is. The most popular form of Energy Psychology used today is "EFT," which stands for "Emotional Freedom Techniques" and is also known as "Tapping." Another common Energy Psychology method is "TFT," which stands for Thought Field Therapy. Energy Psychology has been around since the late 1970s but it has only started to become more popular over the past 5-10 years. So it's also possible that you haven't heard of it before.

There are lots of people who dabble in Energy Psychology techniques and get good or mixed results. However, when these processes are used comprehensively by a skilled practitioner, they produce miraculous change. When I work with clients, I always practice Comprehensive Energy Psychology and it produces deep long-lasting results that are sometimes astonishing.

What Energy Psychology Is and Why It Works

Energy Psychology is a collection of mind-body approaches that can improve your well-being in many ways. The traditional Western medical model is based on Newtonian science, which is now considered to be outdated. People are realizing this more and more and turning to holistic methods based on the new sciences instead.

The fact that our world is accepting this new science and adapting to it is a wonderful thing. I believe that it means we have evolved to a new and deeper understanding of the Universe and human condition. We live in a quantum world, and everything is made up of atoms. Atoms are made of energy. Anything in our life can shift and change at any time because everything is energy. That gives us infinite possibilities as to what can happen in our life.

The energetic frequency in our body is the foundation of our health. Our body contains energy pathways and centers that are in constant communication with our mind, organs, and cells. Every thought and emotion that we experience causes a reaction in a specific area of your brain. Brain imaging devices, such as a PET scanner, show us that this is true.

Every experience in life creates an energetic vibration that is stored in our body. When the experience is disturbing, that vibration may cause negative thoughts, which lead to negative thought patterns and negative feelings.

The tissues in our body can become affected by negative energy and issues related to your mental health or general health could develop as a result of that. Energy Psychology allows us to release this vibration that does not serve our greater good. And not only can we release it, we can add more of what we do want into our system, which means that we can change *anything* we wish to change. Through Energy Psychology, we actually have the power to re-write our lives!

More and more evidence is showing the true power and potential of these methods. People once questioned whether the 16 energy meridians of the body actually existed. Now we know that they exist because they have been photographed.

And there are now over 100 reputable studies published that indicate energy psychology methods are effective 98% of the time. Compare that to the outcomes in traditional Western treatment methods, many of which are successful only 50-60% of the time. I believe it will replace medicine and many of our traditional treatment methods at some point in the future.

I feel it's important that we see ourselves as energetic beings, because when we do, the possibilities for ourselves and our lives are limitless. Energy can shift and change at any time, which means that we can also! We have the ability to release what is not serving our greatest good and we can choose instead to absorb the frequencies and vibrations that we would prefer to have. We have the ability to constantly evolve in every area of our life. By acknowledging ourselves as energetic beings, we step into our power knowing that all is possible!

How exciting that our world has just started to acknowledge this new science that supports unlimited possibilities for our lives!

"All truth passes through three stages. First it is ridiculed. Second, it is violently opposed. Third, it is accepted as self-evident."
– Arthur Schopenhauer, Philosopher

Energy Psychology helped Jill clear her subconscious blocks. I don't think Jill is an exception to the rule; I think she's actually a great example of the rule. We frequently find ourselves with actions and behaviors that don't match up with what we consciously want.

This misalignment is also the root of Self-Sabotage. We say we want to lose 10 lbs., then we go out for ice cream. We say we want to save some money, then go online and start buying things. Those are two examples of how we sabotage ourselves when our conscious and subconscious minds are not in alignment.

Why would these parts of your mind not be in alignment with one another? One of the main reasons I've found is that a huge component of our unconscious mind comes from our childhood. During the course of our childhood, we draw conclusions and make judgments about ourselves and our life experiences because we want the world to make sense. But some of these conclusions are wrong and there's no one else in our mind to correct them for us.

The conclusions that we draw about life at these young ages often become subconscious beliefs that are stored in our mind and we forget about them. Later in life, these beliefs play out as life patterns and we have no idea why their particular theme keeps repeating in our life. But there's actually a very good reason. We have subconscious beliefs creating them.

Let's just say for example your mother told you many times in childhood that it's not safe to talk to strangers. Then one day when you were eight years old, you were walking home from the bus stop and a stranger in a car stopped to talk to you. Your mom had just seen on the news that there's a strange man who has been in the neighborhood trying to pick up young children. Your mom is now even more watchful of you than she usually is after hearing this on the news because she's worried.

As you are walking home from the bus stop she comes outside and sees that you are talking to the stranger. She immediately yells at you to stop talking to the stranger and commands you to go directly in the house because you are now in trouble as she's told you numerous times not to do this.

When you get in the house, your mom tells you that you're grounded for two weeks. This means that you have to miss your best friend's birthday party. You are so disappointed that you start to believe in your mind that "talking to strangers is the worst thing to do." You think about this over and over again consciously, but eventually it absorbs into your subconscious and you don't realize that you still have this belief.

Your behavior around strangers starts to change as a result of carrying this belief. Now you are shy when you're around them. It becomes hard to talk to new teachers at school.

As an adult this makes social gatherings and job interviews very uncomfortable, but that old experience is stored in your mind from long ago and you no longer remember it. You rationalize your social anxiety as, "I just don't like making small talk with new people." But subconsciously there is a perfect explanation for this that you are not even aware of.

We are constantly trying to understand the world around us, so we create beliefs about it based on our experiences. If we like our experience, the beliefs that we develop about it will be positive and help us in life. But for our experiences that we don't like, we develop beliefs that may limit us or hold us back. And in some cases, they can even cause harm.

We have at least 70,000 thoughts per day. Some people have up to 90,000 per day! If you do the math, that's at least one thought per second, in some cases it's more than one. Because we have so many thoughts, we aren't conscious of many of them because we are having multiple at the same time. In fact, we can even have polar opposite thoughts almost simultaneously. A lot of people don't know this.

These constant thoughts that are occurring in our mind are a mixture of old and new, but the old are more constant and repetitive. When we experience a lot of emotional disturbance about a present situation, it is usually because it is activating old similar thoughts and beliefs that are always present but not always noticed.

We might think that the emotional pain we're feeling is related to the present moment, but really it's more about the old unresolved pain that is getting rubbed by the present similar experience. That's one of the reasons why it's so important to access your subconscious mind through methods like muscle testing (Applied Kinesiology) when you are in your healing process.

When you experience traumatic grief, it's important to figure out which old wounds are being activated by the loss that you're experiencing. This is an important part of healing your grief. Without it, your healing won't be complete.

An example of this could be that you experienced a loss early in life that has been affecting you unconsciously since it happened. Maybe you were so young when it happened, it didn't appear to have much of an effect on you. But it did, and this new loss is showing you that this old wound needs to heal also.

Life is always trying to help us, whether we think that it

is or not. Part of the depth of the pain you are experiencing is the Universe letting you know that you have more to heal than just this loss.

Energy Psychology gives you a way to heal all of your wounds easily and profoundly.

Chapter 5

Loss and Love

While it's obvious that a big part of the grief Kristin felt was because she had a beautiful relationship with her father and she loved him very much, it really wasn't obvious that her relationship with herself also played a role in her grief.

Neither Kristin nor I had any idea that our relationship with our Self had anything to do with the deep emotional pain that we couldn't get out of. But as it turned out for both of us, it was playing a huge role. Your relationship with your Self always comes into play when dealing with any type of loss, be it a death or some other type.

Our relationship with our Self is no different than any other relationship in the Universe, in that it is rooted in Love. It took me a while into my healing journey to realize that all relationships at their core are rooted in love. Sometimes a relationship doesn't appear to have the presence of love in it, but that's only because there is something blocking the Love that is present. Love is the building block of the Universe.

Step 3: R – Revitalize Your Self-Love and Spirituality

Contrary to popular belief, Self-Love has nothing to do with how pretty you think you are, nor does it have anything to do with being a Narcissist. In fact, Narcissistic traits are actually the opposite of Self-Love. But that's a whole different book lol.

It's also much deeper than just liking yourself or thinking you're a decent person. Love goes much deeper than like. Self-Love is about feeling whole and complete in and with the deepest part of our being.

When we feel whole and complete with who we are deep inside, we develop a bond with our Self. In a sense, it's almost like naturally becoming your own best friend. You make good, healthy choices for yourself and in any situation, you have your own back. You trust your decisions and judgment, just like you would trust those of your best friend. How often do you treat yourself like your own best friend?

When we feel like there is something about us that is wrong or unworthy, that shows up in our life as well. It shows up in our relationships, our job and career, our health, the way we take care of ourselves and the way we manage our time.

Look at these areas of your life: Relationships, Career, Health, Self-Care, Time Management. Is there anything that needs to change?

It's easy to not realize that you aren't loving yourself as much as you deserve to. That's because as children we are taught to love other people, but very few of us have been taught how to love our self. The idea of self-love, what it is and how we can strengthen it is a fairly new concept. But even if you were taught, you can still always go deeper and love yourself more.

In childhood, you grow up with adults preparing you to live in a crazy and dysfunctional world. You were taught to work hard, be productive, achieve, and don't get in trouble. They truly meant well with those lessons. And they did that because that's what they knew to do. They repeated what they were taught.

But the world is evolving, and we've now neglected our heart for so long that it is calling for our attention louder than ever.

In this world of instant gratification, it's easy to cover the discomfort in our heart. We turn to multiple vices – food, alcohol and shopping are just a few of the most common ways we seek to change our internal state or seek fulfillment. But it only works temporarily. Because there is no external solution for an internal problem.

When you have a strong and loving bond with your Self, life makes more sense. The more life makes sense, the more you can trust life. The more you trust life, the more you can connect with your Divine gifts. We all have divine gifts that we are here to share with the world. In sharing our Divine gifts, we start to develop a deeper sense of purpose, joy, fulfillment, and peace.

The Role of Self-Love in Traumatic Grief

Love is the Truth of who we are. We come from the Divine source which is essentially Love. When we are not in the state of love or feeling unloved, something is blocking us from that. Your body's Love center is your heart. In your heart lies your Truth.

When a loss results in deep emotional pain that you can't seem to get beyond, part of the reason is because you've been depending on that person's Love. The reason you've been depending on that person's Love is because you are not fully extending your own Love to yourself. So while the pain feels brand new, some of it has been in existence for a long time.

In order to love yourself fully, your heart must be fully open. When your heart is more closed than open, it limits the flow of Love in your life.

There are many reasons why you may have closed your heart and are not loving yourself fully. One the most common reasons I see has to do with trust.

Somewhere in your past you had an experience and you decided that it's not safe to trust yourself or other people. So you closed your heart in an attempt to protect yourself. But the thinking that led you to close your heart came from your Ego mind and is not for your greatest good. I'll talk about Ego in the next chapter.

In Kristin's case, she had closed her heart considerably, and one of the few people she stayed open to was her dad. It's no wonder why her world was crushed when he passed. She had to really work hard to open her heart to herself so she could feel whole again not having him in her life. But she stayed with the hard work and it paid off for her big time.

Learning to trust will help you to keep your heart open, which is essential for Self-Love and loving others which, at its core, is one and the same and essential for your healing journey.

A Course in Miracles states, "Only what *you* have not given can be lacking in any situation."

Strengthening Self-Love

While Love is the building block of the Universe, we live in a world that rarely acknowledges it. We frequently make meanings out of situations and events that provoke negative, fear-based feelings about life and the world around us that disturb us, rather than making positive meanings of these situations that would provoke positive, love-based emotion and a sense of peace.

Fears, beliefs, and judgments are just some of your blocks to Self-Love. Many have come from childhood and have been reinforced in adulthood. Consciously, you may know only a few of them, but many exist for all of us, without exception.

The good news here is that you have the power to change anything in your life that's not working for you, and Self-Love is no exception. Comprehensive Energy Psychology allows you to let go of your blocks to Self-Love and install the new information that supports your highest good.

When you begin to identify these blocks, some will be conscious and you will recognize them right away. But there will also be many others that are subconscious. Some of the subconscious information could be very surprising when you access your subconscious and see what's actually there. My clients are always surprised when I muscle test them for beliefs they don't think they have and it turns out that they do actually have them.

Some of the most common of these beliefs that I see in my clients are:

- I'm not enough.
- I'm not good enough.
- I'm not a good enough _____.
- I'm not successful enough.
- I'm not smart enough.
- I'm not accepted by others.
- I'm not well liked.
- I'm not well loved.
- I don't deserve _____.

After you clear the core beliefs you've identified, whether it be the ones identified from above, others, or both, you will want to install and/or strengthen positive beliefs to enhance and further develop your sense of Self-Love.

In some cases, you will want to install the exact opposite of the belief you released. In other cases, a belief similar to the opposite of the belief will work just as well.

Some examples of these beliefs could be:

- I am enough.
- I'm good enough.
- I'm more than enough.

- I am successful.
- I deserve lots of success.
- I'm very smart and people notice my brilliance.
- I am well liked.
- I am well loved.
- I deserve a life that I love.

Fears and judgments can be cleared similarly to beliefs, although you wouldn't install new ones (obviously! Lol).

Some common examples of Fears:

- Fear of Not Being Good Enough
- Fear of Not Being Successful
- Fear of Being Successful
- Fear of Not Being Liked
- Fear of Not Being Loved
- Fear of Not Deserving What I Want

Some common examples of Judgments:

- I'm not pretty/handsome enough.
- I'm not the right weight.
- I'm not the right height.
- My (body part) is too big/ too small.
- I haven't accomplished _____.
- I'm not good at _____.
- I'm bad at _____.
- I failed at _____.

(Perfectionism is also sign that you are judging yourself frequently.)

Reflection

As human beings, for many of us Self-Love is not our strong suit, and that's OK. But if you want to heal from your grief and improve your life overall dramatically, developing more Self-Love is an important part of your recipe.

If you really want to gauge your level of Self-Love, get a full assessment in your Grief Cure Toolkit at TheGriefCure.com.

Here is a short exercise to start assessing yourself:

On a scale of 0-10, with 0 being never and 10 being extremely true, rate the following statements. At the end of the statements, add up your score.

1. I am kind to myself always.
2. I am always compassionate to myself when I make errors.
3. I am always happy with my body.
4. I have unconditional love for every part of my body.
5. All of the relationships in my life are supportive of my needs.
6. I lovingly put my self-care first.

Find out more about your score and get your full Grief Cure toolkit at TheGriefCure.com, which includes a complete assessment on self-love!

Questions for More Reflection:

1. How often do you treat yourself like your own best friend?

2. Look at these areas of your life: Relationships, Career, Health, Self-Care, Time management. If your life was your best friend's, what advice would you give her or him?

3. Did any of the example negative beliefs resonate with you? If so, which one(s)?

4. Did any of the example Fears resonate with you? If so, which ones?

5. Do you judge yourself in any of the ways listed?

Chapter 6

Ego

When we look at the great religions of the world, their teachings all have one common theme: Love. So if all of the greatest spiritual teachings are essentially about love, then our higher source – whether you consider it to be God, Source, Energy, or something else, must be loving in nature. Therefore, all that is created in life is done so in love. Are you with me?

With God being all-loving and all-powerful, he (or she) would want us to be the most loving beings we can be, therefore he would create experiences for us that would help us to evolve in this way and open our heart rather than close it, would he not?

This means that the life experiences our higher source brings to us are always born out of the intention to make us more loving than we currently are. To judge these life experiences as bad or a result of punishment would only result in you closing yourself to the opportunity that has been brought to you, to love more. When you close to the opportunity, you create the need for the higher intelligence of the Universe to bring you yet another experience to open your heart more.

All of our experiences – regardless of how our mortal mind has labeled them – good, bad, or otherwise – are actually intended for us to become a more loving person. From a Divine standpoint, the purpose of pain is to rise beyond it, so you may grow and become a wiser and more loving version of you.

In other words, the purpose of pain is actually peace. Pain is here to help us. To call our attention to things in our life that need to change. It is in pain that we become open to healing. And healing is what we are here to do in this lifetime. So, believe it or not, pain has value.

Traumatic Grief is an opportunity to grow and expand our hearts and minds in new ways we'd never have done otherwise. It's through this deep emotional pain and discomfort that might even feel like you "hit rock bottom" that motivates you to see and do things differently. As we break down, we are actually opening up.

It can be hard to wrap your head around the possibility of something really good coming out of a devastating experience, because the paradigm of the world says otherwise. But this is where you shift your paradigm to remember the Higher Truth of who you are. If you are open to this possibility, it surely will happen. But you must be open.

Part of being open and shifting your paradigm means recognizing that there is always a bigger, broader perspective than what your mortal mind sees. There is a higher intention that your mortal mind doesn't understand because it's attached to the outcome you want. And the outcome you want is based on a tiny part of an enormous picture.

It is from this bigger, broader perspective that the algorithms of the Universe are created. That's why life doesn't always make sense. This loss that you're experiencing is part of an algorithm that has a higher plan for your life. We don't change when we are comfortable. And the Universe knows this. Your emotional pain is a giant nudge.

When we can see Grief as merely an algorithm of the Universe, it's no longer a meaningless experience. It has value. And as strange as it may sound, this experience is here to help us step into the next best version of ourselves. We can use this experience as a tool to help us step into our life in a whole new way.

The Role of the Ego in Traumatic Grief

The main reason why we often don't understand the lessons that the Universe is bringing to us, such as Grief, is because of a part of our mind called the Ego. The Ego is a part of our subconscious mind that induces suffering because it is trying to protect our body. This is an old part of our reptilian brain that sees us only as physical beings and doesn't acknowledge our spiritual nature.

It might sound strange that there would be a part of your mind that is designed to promote suffering, but when you think about the nature of life, thousands (if not millions) of years ago, it makes perfect sense. At that point in human evolution, life for human beings was very different and we developed this part of our mind in order to protect ourselves.

For example, if you got attacked by a tiger, you would want to stay far away from tigers. Your Ego would hold on to that traumatic memory and your life-threatening experience so whenever you see something that even slightly reminds you of a tiger, you will avoid it at all costs.

But at this point in human evolution, we don't need that part of our mind. And in some cases, it can actually cause harm to us because we make decisions about our life while thinking with this part of our brain that is meant to create and hold on to suffering. When I teach my clients what Ego thoughts are, they are often amazed by how many Ego thoughts they are having daily and how strong of a hold this part of their mind has on them.

One of my clients a few years ago came to me suffering extreme anxiety and depression due to an abundance of Ego thoughts. I immediately started working with her to shift from the fear-based Ego thinking to love-based spiritual thinking and her world began shifting quickly. In just four months, 75% of the emotional and physical symptoms she had reported at our first session were resolved.

It has been estimated that our Ego mind is currently 15-18x more active than we need it to be at this point in human evolution. I think of our Ego mind in a sense, as like our wisdom teeth, except teeth can be surgically removed.

The Ego can't be removed, but its power can be greatly decreased. Being aware of its presence and being aware of Ego driven thoughts are two ways to lessen its power. In your Grief cure toolbox at TheGriefCure.com you will find an Ego Mind inventory to help you identify Ego thoughts you may be having that could be harmful to your wellbeing.

The Ego Plays Two Main Roles in Traumatic Grief:
1. **It holds on to the pain.**

The Ego holds onto the pain you're experiencing in an attempt to prevent this type of occurrence from happen again, however, it makes no sense because this pain is part of a spiritual lesson that we are experiencing, that we need to have for our soul growth.

2. **You forget that you and your loved one are eternal.**
The Ego mind is designed to protect our body at all costs, so when the Ego is dominating our thought patterns we can easily forget that we are not just a body.

That forgetting plays a role in Traumatic Grief because when we don't realize the role our Ego is playing in this equation, we will just hold on to the pain and forget our truth, which is that we are not just a body.

We are beings of infinite potential experiencing a spiritual lesson that the Universe has brought especially for us. We are not just a body walking around planet Earth as the Ego believes.

This means that our loved ones are eternal as well, and we have not lost them, our relationship has just changed form.

When we keep in mind that we are spiritual beings, loss doesn't even exist. Grief is part of the struggle between knowing the truth of who you are and your Ego telling you that you are a body with no Divine purpose.

Dr. Brian Weiss says, "We are immortal beings who are never energetically separated from those we love. We have eternal soulmates and soul families. We are never alone. We often forget that we, as souls, experience lifetimes in physical bodies, but we are not those bodies."

It's important to resist the urge from the Ego to close your heart, shrink, and blame others for what has happened. This is a fear-based reaction that comes from Ego thinking and it will keep you stuck for however long you choose to make that your reality.

Spiritual Development

When Kristin dealt with the loss of her father, she had absolutely no sense of Spirituality. This left her with no substantial framework to understand both what had actually happened to her father and what she was experiencing emotionally.

Was he at the cemetery? Was he in heaven? Could her dog see him? Was he visiting her in dreams? Her children asked questions about him and she would create answers to the questions, but never really felt certain that she believed her own answers. She felt very troubled by that.

As Kristin began to heal and become curious about her spiritual nature, she realized that she didn't need to follow an organized religion to develop a belief system that would both help her heal her pain and prevent her from ever having to deal with such confusion and heartbreak ever again. And as she began to develop herself spiritually, her life began to transform

Chapter 7

What Next?

A coral reef that is exposed at low tide was not created by the low tide; it was covered by water prior to the change of tide. What makes traumatic grief different from other types of grief is that it exposes all of the issues that were living under the surface. The exposure of these deeper issues has sometimes been called "The Low Tide Effect."

It doesn't feel good to have all of these issues exposed, and it might even seem overwhelming, considering that you're deeply bereaved on top of these other issues. But I assure you that this is an important discovery, and it's actually an opportunity. The Universe has shown you the exact issues that need to heal and change, and I'm teaching you the recipe that will help you to accomplish this. This is the perfect setup to start making life changes.

Step 4: E – Envision a Transformed Life and Take Action

In order to start creating change in your life, you need to develop some vision so you know what you are working toward. I suggest you begin with a clear starting point and allow it to change and evolve for the better as you change and evolve on your journey of transformation.

As you evolve to the next best version of your Self, your vision will naturally evolve also. You want to always have a life vision that is substantially bigger and more exciting than what's happening in your life right now.

For me, I like to make big goals, then figure out the steps that will lead me to achieve my goals. Then I start taking action right away. Many of my clients have found that this method works well for them also.

In order to start creating your vision, you'll need to go deep into your heart because that's where your Truth is. There are many ways that you can move deeply into your heart. In your Grief Cure Toolkit (at TheGriefCure.com) I have a few exercises that will help you to get clarity about your new life vision.

But before you go online, let's start off with a brief exercise to drop into your heart center, then you can answer and reflect on some questions that will help you with your new life vision. You'll want to use a separate piece of paper and pen for the writing portion of this exercise, so feel free to go grab that right now.

Now that you have your paper and pen, I want you to sit down in a very comfortable position. If you are sitting, you'll want to either be sitting in a chair with your feet on the floor and spine straight, or you could sit on the floor or a bed in Lotus Position. Once you are sitting, close your eyes and take some slow deep breaths, inhaling through your nose and exhaling through your mouth with pursed lips. After about 4-5 breaths, you can start the process of dropping down into your heart with this Heart Consciousness Exercise.

Exercise: Heart Consciousness

1. Close your eyes.
2. Take some slow deep breaths
3. Imagine yourself surrounded by a divine golden light that is here to love and protect you. This same golden light is now shining down on you as well, entering your body through the crown of your head, then moving slowly through your body, covering every space and every organ. It moves completely through you all the way down to your feet,

then it travels through your feet and back into the earth.

4. After your internal state becomes filled with this loving divine light, you begin to notice your heart, and the divine light that continues to be present here.

5. You enter inside your heart and notice the great depth of love, compassion, generosity, and kindness that dwell here. There is an everlasting well of goodness that resides here. And it is waiting to serve your highest good and intentions.

6. And as you use your conscious awareness to discover all of this goodness residing in your heart chakra and center, you slowly lower this consciousness downward and into your heart. And with your consciousness in your heart center, you are now able to envision your life from your heart-centered Truth.

Creating an Exciting New Vision for Your Life

If you had a magic wand that could grant you anything in your life that you wished for, what would it be?

Health and Well-being

- What would be vibrant health for you?

Relationships and Love
- What do your ideal friendships entail?
- What do your ideal relationships entail?

Vocation and Creation
- What is your mission in life?
- What would you love to create in the world?
- What kind of career would make you jump for joy?

Now, write your answers to these questions on a paper.

Re-read the paper a few times.

Close your eyes and visualize for 2-3 minutes what it would be like to live this life.

How does it feel to imagine this new life?

Please write 2-4 sentences on your paper that describe how you feel when you close your eyes and imagine this life.

Now let's take a look at your current life. Please write down what you're experiencing in your life right now. Take a few minutes to examine the following areas:

-Health and Well-being

-Relationships and Love

-Vocation and Creation

Now let's reflect by looking at both your current life and your new life vision:

- How close are you to your new life vision? Rate on a scale from 1-10 with 10 being you are actually living your vision.
- How much do you want this new life? On a scale from 1-10 with 10 being the maximum, please rate your desire.
- How committed are you to actually making this new life happen? On a scale of 1-10 with 10 the maximum, what is your level of commitment?

If your level of commitment to this change is an 8 or higher, that's a very good sign! You can totally have all of the things in your life that you listed (plus more)! You just need to do the work required to release your blocks to creating and manifesting this new life.

The fact that we are, at our core, energetic beings living in a Quantum Universe, means we have unlimited possibilities and potential for our life. All of the blocks that we face are some form of energy – you just need to identify what the blocks are and release them.

It may sound too simple, that you can let go of anything standing in the way of your goals, but it really is true! The evidence is in both my life and the lives of my clients.

And that's actually why a lot of people don't do this, because it sounds really simple! Some people think it's too good to be true, because we've been taught our whole life that life is complicated and there are some things that can't be changed. But that couldn't be further from the Truth. Anyone who believes this simply doesn't know how to tap into their power to create limitless change.

It really is a new concept that you can change anything in your life that doesn't serve you, but that's only because the science behind it is new. As the new science becomes utilized more, which seems to be happening already, these concepts will become a part of our paradigm.

A Course in Miracles suggests that the most successful people in the world have only tapped into a small fraction of their full potential, which means that the average person is nowhere near their potential.

Imagine that—the celebrities, gurus, and experts—that most people only aspire to be like—have only tapped into a small fraction of what they are capable of. That might be hard to believe, but it's actually true.

I wholeheartedly believe this to be true because I received confirmation of this in a workshop I did last year.

In this workshop, I used muscle testing (Applied Kinesiology) to gauge where people were in relation to their full potential. I had people guess where they thought they were, and then used muscle testing to see if they were correct.

The results were surprising for everyone. Most people guessed that they were between 30-50% of their full potential. And when I checked them with muscle testing, the majority came out between 3-5%! Not one person guessed correctly and nearly everyone was astonished by their result.

So imagine that. You are probably at less than 10% of your life potential!

We have a tendency to live in a smaller expression of ourselves and not step into what is really possible because so much of our daily thinking comes from the Ego, and the Ego holds onto pain and suffering. So we tend to have thoughts and plans that keep us "thinking little" and within our comfort zone, which is what's familiar to us.

But unfortunately, there is no growth in life without some

discomfort. If you think back to your best accomplishments in life, at some point in your journey to get there, I guarantee that you experienced some discomfort.

If your level of commitment to change from the exercise on p.76 is under an 8, you're probably experiencing a lot of thoughts that are Ego-based and not coming from your Truth. If this is the case, it's important to do some reflection here so you don't stay stuck.

Some questions you may want to reflect upon are:

1. Do you believe that it's possible to create an exciting new life?
2. Do you believe that you deserve to create an exciting new life?
3. Do you believe that it's safe to create an exciting new life?
4. Do you believe that you will do what it takes to create an exciting new life?
5. Do you believe that you'll lose something important if you let go of what's going on in your life right now and take action toward creating an exciting new life?

If you answered "no" or "maybe" to any of those questions, your Ego is definitely playing a role here and trying to keep you stuck. It's likely that you have somehow become used to your life as it is, and you might even have beliefs about it not being possible to change into a way of living that you deeply enjoy.

It's also possible that you are feeling "uncomfortably comfortable," which is what happens when you desire change in your life, but the action required to make the changes you desire feels more uncomfortable than the discomfort you are currently feeling.

Whatever the case may be, just knowing that the only thing holding you back from the changes you want to make is thoughts that are coming from your Ego mind, can be a very empowering piece of knowledge!

Because you now know that you can start changing whenever you choose to do so, you are developing a new awareness. And with this awareness, the unconscious cycle of not knowing is broken.

You can now start living consciously and in your Truth, knowing that it's merely self-sabotaging thoughts – nothing at all of substance – just thoughts – that are getting in the way of you living out your heart's desires.

Everyone has one, if not many, life purposes. You are not here in life randomly – the Universe knew what it was doing when it invited you to be here! And it wasn't so you could be sad, unfulfilled, or unhappy. So step into your power and

take action toward the life that the Universe is begging you
to create!

> *"You are light beyond light, you are love beyond love,*
> *you are a beautiful vessel of infinite possibilities that is*
> *bringing this whole world home."*
> – Rikka Zimmerman

Chapter 8

Challenges

You now have the key ingredients to completely heal from the grief and other issues that you're experiencing. Now it's your job to cook them up and make a masterpiece! The Grief Cure Method is powerful and profound. It will change your life like nothing before it. This means that it's going to take some work that is not for the faint of heart. But you are meant to do this work and deep down you know it. The Universe is calling you to step up and live life at a whole new level and you can feel it.

If you choose to follow these four steps as a guide to heal your grief, you will get much more than that. Your life will start opening up in ways that you never imagined. Unbelievable opportunities and coincidences will suddenly start appearing for you. Your life will start shifting into a clear new direction that excites you. This is the Universe's way of telling you that you're on track and to keep moving at full speed.

Along with living a life that excites and inspires you, your relationships will start changing in positive ways and your level of inner peace will deepen. You will eventually become so strong and in sync with life that you will become unshakable and will never have to worry about dealing with heartbreaking grief or being afraid of "something bad" happening. You will have complete faith in life with an unshakable sense of peace.

But like anything in life, change can be uncomfortable. And you're venturing into issues that are uncharted territory for you. So I'd like to go over some of the challenges you will likely come across in your process.

Resistance

Resistance is a natural part of the process when it comes to making changes and moving forward in your life. Sometimes I like to think of change and resistance as the Yin and the Yang, because one doesn't exist without the other. It can come in many forms and the bigger the change, the stronger the resistance. And it's usually quite sneaky. In most cases I've seen, it presents itself as something that doesn't appear to be resistance. It could be forgetting to do something you planned, misplacing your book, or having a headache or poor sleep that impacts your ability to work on something important. It can be almost anything that prevents you from really devoting yourself to the change that you're committed to making. Some people have described resistance as feeling like you're driving with one foot on the gas and the other foot on the brake.

The reason you'll probably have a lot of resistance is because your Ego is used to running the show. It speaks first and loudest and, up until now, you probably didn't even realize that this voice isn't helpful, so you've been following it pretty often. When you start making these changes to step into a higher version of yourself, the Ego will have a lot to say about that and may consciously or unconsciously try to talk you out of this change. And its sneakiness is real! Think about how many people you know talk about making a change or doing something different that would be beneficial and how many of them actually follow through. Everyone who hasn't followed through has been allowing the Ego to influence their decisions.

That little voice can easily trick you. That's one of the reasons why I get really excited whenever a new client signs up to work with me. Many people try to make changes and struggle to make the smallest step forward because of this resistance that most people don't even know exists. But because I've seen the Ego use every trick in its hat, I know exactly how to handle each trick. My clients never have to worry about not knowing what to do when they're facing resistance, so they never slip through this crack. When someone signs up to work with me, it's near guaranteed that they will get the results they want.

Between resistance and the busyness of life in general, it's very easy to get sidetracked when making important life changes, which is why I recommend working with a coach, mentor, or therapist who will hold you accountable to your commitment and desire for change. Using a friend as an accountability partner can work sometimes also. I myself have invested in coaches, mentors, and therapists during important times of my own transition and I wouldn't be where I am today without them.

Another challenge of working independently is that we can help ourselves only as far as we ourselves can see. We have lots of unconscious patterns and issues that we don't know even exist because we are so used to having them. They have a big hold on us because we don't even know what they are. It's likely that these issues are affecting you even more than the issues that you already know you have. Working with someone will help you to find these blind spots so you can be free of these issues for good.

Aside from the voice of the Ego, it's important to recognize how challenging it is to make changes in your life in general. That's why over 90% of New Year's Resolutions don't get completed.

It's now been proven that your brain can change over time and Energy Psychology methods can speed this process up, but you have to be devoted to making this change, otherwise you could easily fall into the 90+% who don't accomplish what they've set out to do.

Another important aspect to acknowledge in this process is to realize that time is not going heal these issues. I tried that myself and saw that it didn't work. I waited six months before attempting to get any support for the horrible emotional pain I was in and it didn't help me one bit.

> *"They always say time changes things, but you actually have to change them yourself."*
> – Andy Warhol

And in this case, it's especially true because grief is an energetic vibration that will be stored in your body until you release it. Energetic vibrations that stay in your body get stored in your tissues and will contribute to the state of your overall health, which is a very good reason to start this work right away.

If you wait to work on these issues, they can become more complex over time. Aside from the fact that I've seen this happen, the Law of Complexity Consciousness states that issues have a tendency to get more complex over time. This means that the sooner you start to make changes, the easier your journey will be.

Another thing that's important to remember is that as soon as you set a strong intention to accomplish something that the Universe wants you to do, it will start rearranging your life to support you. This might or might not be what you're expecting. It's going to show you everything that's in your way of getting where you want to go. And it might be more than you expected.

Some people get overwhelmed when these unexpected blocks come up and in some cases, you could think it's a signal to quit, but the Universe knows that you're capable of facing and resolving these issues, otherwise it would not have brought them up for you. You must surrender to the process, which can be a challenge all on its own.

I can say from my own experience, the journey of healing from many deep wounds and releasing countless inner blocks is not a straight line going forward. There will be days that you can feel yourself growing in leaps and bounds, but there will also be days when you question yourself and wonder if the hard days will ever end. At the beginning of your journey, you'll expect the latter more than the former, so having support is crucial.

But the further you go into your journey, the easier it will be. Once the core issues have been resolved, everything will get much easier, generally speaking. Personal growth is an important part of the life journey and if you think of it as a hobby you enjoy, it will be a much easier journey.

Transformation is a journey and not a destination. I believe that Transformation is meant to be a part of our life. The human race has finally evolved enough. We have the resources, skills, and knowledge to make leveling up to the next best version of yourself something you can do regularly. So why not do it? I feel we have a responsibility to ourselves and the world to always be evolving into our next best self. And remember, you don't have to do it alone. The people who supported me on my journey, both personal friends and healing professionals, were essential to my transformation. So, embrace the ones who will be a part of yours.

"The pain pushes until the vision pulls."
– Michael Bernard Beckwith

Conclusion

One of the most important things that I've learned in my journey out of painful grief and into a life of deep inner peace and happiness that I didn't even know was possible is that nothing in the Universe happens randomly. It's a distinct algorithm and all is in perfect sync. However, you must be open to seeing the possibilities beyond what your mortal mind can comprehend in order to really grasp this concept.

Figuring out this truth was not a quick or easy task. It took me years to start connecting the dots and making some sense out of my life. I would've sworn that the Universe was random and had no purpose in its rhythms.

So much of it didn't make sense to me. But that was because I was looking at tiny pieces of the Universal puzzle and not understanding the ways in which everything connects.

The reason I wrote this book and created The Grief Cure Method is so that no one ever has to suffer through the horrific pain of traumatic grief – feeling completely lost and wondering month after month, year after year, if you'll ever get back to being the person you once were.

I've been that person. And although I now see the value in my journey through the pain, I'd love to help anyone I can to not have to go through that experience.

This program contains the essential pieces that need to change within you so you can heal and change your life for the better without having to figure it all out on your own like I did.

Not only will The Grief Cure Method get you back to who you were, it will take you far beyond that old identity to places that you didn't even know you wanted to go.

This is an opportunity to change your life in a huge way. Yes, it will take resources like time, money, and patience. But I can tell you from my own personal experience, that the outcome is worth double your investment, if not more.

Nothing worthwhile in life has a quick fix and this is no exception. The Universe is begging you to do this work. The cosmos has aligned for you to take this huge leap forward in your life. And if you say yes to this opportunity, the blessings and miracles that are in store for you will blow your mind.

You already know that trying to stuff your feelings doesn't work. Your True Self won't let you stuff them because it knows you have important work to do.

If you respond to this calling as you are meant to do, you will open yourself up to see the many blessings that are meant to come out of this. I can honestly say, that looking back on everything I went through when my father passed, it had to happen to get me where I am today.

Today I'm living my life purpose and helping people transform their lives in ways that they didn't even know were possible. If I hadn't had to save myself from the abyss of sadness I was drowning in after my father's death, I wouldn't be here right now, writing a book that I hope will help thousands, if not millions, of people.

Not everyone chooses to work on themselves. Not everyone feels compelled to be the best version of their self that they can be. But some of us do. And it's not that we came up with that idea on our own, something has led us to the path.

All you need to do is start walking forward. Follow these steps. Use your intuition. Embark on this journey and your path will naturally unfold. The GPS of the cosmos will guide you on your way at every turn.

"It takes courage to endure the sharp pains of self-discovery, rather than choose to take the dull pain of unconsciousness that would last the rest of our lives."
– Marianne Williamson

Be the brave soul that you are here to be!

Acknowledgments

There are many people who supported me on the journey that led to writing this book. I have several friends, family, clients, coaches, and healers who have been a part of the journey to my arrival here and I deeply honor each one of you.

To my paternal grandparents who raised me to believe I was special.

To my dad who helped me to develop into the unique person I am today who wrote this book.

Many thank you's to my Aunt "Carol" who is also my godmother and supports me in all that I do.

I send huge gratitude hugs to Henry Grayson, for the amazing work that he has brought into this world, his commitment to share it to promote healing. He has also taught me a great deal about how to be loving and kind. Both he and Linda Busk have been important mentors in my life that helped me to heal and see the world the way that I needed to see it in order to write this book. I send giant hugs to Linda as well!

My great friend Carolyn Goodrich has certainly been a big encourager on this journey. She believes in everything that I do, helps me to think big, and is always ready to accompany me on a personal growth adventure wherever it may take us.

Of course, I can't leave out my Paradigm Shift Team. I'm so blessed to have you all.

To my dear friend Waleska who was my first assistant and sister in a past life. She helped and supported me through my earliest days and has always been full of encouragement – ready to help at a moment's notice.

To all of my friends of many years who helped me in the hardest year of my life (2009-2010): Lynda Farouk, Donna Huber, and Jonté Allen especially. Thank you for your love and support and helping me to maintain my sanity.

And of course, to my loyal friend Mike Cerullo, who has always believed in me and the work I do and supported me on some of my darkest days of grief.

To Laura Hosford – thank you for confirming my feeling that it was almost time to write a book!

To the Morgan James Publishing team: Special thanks to David Hancock, CEO & Founder for believing in me and my message. To my Author Relations Manager, Bonnie Rauch, thanks for making the process seamless and easy. Many more thanks to everyone else, but especially Jim Howard, Bethany Marshall, and Nickcole Watkins.

And I must acknowledge my clients, as they inspire me every day and help me to always remember my lifetime purpose.

Thank You

I just want to extend a huge thank you to you for reading my book! I am so proud of you for getting to this page! There are no coincidences in life, and the fact that you are on this page right now means that you're ready for your next step: my thank-you gift to you for reading my book!

Because I know what it's like to be stuck in the land of heartbreak and not know what to do next, I've designed a toolkit to help you get clarity. Use it to discover where you are and whether you're ready to start your journey to healing all of your pain completely and transforming your grief into your best life ever.

So please go to TheGriefCure.com so you can download your toolkit and start getting clarity about what to do next. You'll be glad you did!

All my love to you!

Alyson

About the Author

Alyson Franz has been helping people transform their lives since 2012 and put the concept of Life Transformation on the map in her home state of Rhode Island when she opened Paradigm Shift, LLC, in 2016. She designs workshops, personal growth programs, and individualized life transformation programs to help clients break-free from grief and trauma, life stressors, and other internal barriers to achieve major personal and life changes in 3-12 months. She is passionate about helping people step into their power, let go of barriers, and live at their true potential.

Alyson has a graduate degree from Simmons College in Boston, Massachusetts, is certified in synergetic therapy by The Synergetic Therapy Institute in New York City and is trained in transformational coaching. She had the privilege of being trained and mentored by several certified Comprehensive Energy Psychology practitioners, including bestselling author, Henry Grayson.

After the sudden loss of her father, Alyson struggled to remake her life. She now uses what she learned at that time, as well as her training, to help others revitalize their lives after loss.

Alyson lives in Johnston, RI, and has several hobbies, including Latin dancing. Alyson speaks Spanish fluently and has been known for her work with the Latino Community in Providence, RI.

www.ParadigmShiftRI.com/
www.Facebook.com/PSLLCRI
www.Instagram.com/paradigmshiftri
www.TheGriefCure.com
www.TheGriefCureBook.com

CPSIA information can be obtained
at www.ICGtesting.com
Printed in the USA
JSHW031325270920
8289JS00001B/112